WHY JEREMIAH SAD?

**The story about Jeremiah is taken from Jeremiah 1; 38:1-13;
II Chronicles 36:15-23; Nehemiah 2.**

*T*hey were angry with Jeremiah and had him beaten and imprisoned in the house of Jonathan the secretary, which they had made into a prison.

Then the officials said to the king, "This man should be put to death. He is discouraging the soldiers who are left in this city, as well as all the people, by the things he is saying to them. This man is not seeking the good of these people but their ruin."

"He is in your hands," King Zedekiah answered. "The king can do nothing to oppose you."

So they took Jeremiah and put him into the cistern of Malkijah, the king's son, which was in the courtyard of the guard. They lowered Jeremiah by ropes into the cistern; it had no water in it, only mud, and Jeremiah sank down into the mud.

But Ebed-Melech, a Cushite, an official in the royal palace, heard that they had put Jeremiah into the cistern. While the king was sitting in the Benjamin Gate, Ebed-Melech went out of the palace and said to him, "My lord the king, these men have acted wickedly in all they have done to Jeremiah the

prophet. They have thrown him into a cistern, where he will starve to death when there is no longer any bread in the city."

Then the king commanded Ebed-Melech the Cushite, "Take thirty men from here with you and lift Jeremiah the prophet out of the cistern before he dies."

So Ebed-Melech took the men with him and went to a room under the treasury in the palace. He took some old rags and worn-out clothes from there and let them down with ropes to Jeremiah in the cistern. Ebed-Melech the Cushite said to Jeremiah, "Put these old rags and worn-out clothes under your arms to pad the ropes." Jeremiah did so, and they pulled him up with the ropes and lifted him out of the cistern. And Jeremiah remained in the courtyard of the guard.

Jeremiah 37:15; 38:4-13, NIV

Why Was Jeremiah Sad?

Published by Scandinavia Publishing House
Nørregade 32, DK-1165 Copenhagen K.
Tel.: (45) 33140091   Fax: (45) 33320091
E-Mail: scanpub1@post4.tele.dk

Copyright © 1997, Pauline Youd
Copyright © on artwork 1997, Daughters of St. Paul
Original English edition published by Pauline Books & Media,
50 Saint Paul's Avenue, Boston, USA
Scripture quotations are from the Holy Bible, New International Version,
Copyright © 1973, 1978, International Bible Society

Design by Ben Alex
Produced by Scandinavia Publishing House

Printed in Singapore.
ISBN 87 7247 031 3

All rights reserved. No part of this book may be reproduced or utilized
in any form or by any means, electronic or mechanical, including
photocopying, recording, or by any information storage and retrieval
system, without permission in writing from the publisher.

WHY WAS JEREMIAH SAD?

By Pauline Youd
Illustrated by Elaine Garvin

SCANDINAVIA

Jeremiah loved to read God's word. He knew it was the truth. It said if people obeyed God they would be happy, but if they disobeyed God they would be punished.

The people around Jeremiah didn't read God's word.

They were unkind and selfish.

They wouldn't help the poor and needy.

"God doesn't see us," they said. That made Jeremiah sad.

God told Jeremiah to tell the people they were disobeying his word.

The people made fun of Jeremiah.

God told Jeremiah to tell them they would be punished.

But the people turned their backs on Jeremiah.

God told Jeremiah to tell them an evil nation would fight against them, capture them, and take them in chains to a faraway country. The people laughed at Jeremiah and said he was crazy, but Jeremiah kept warning them.

The people punished Jeremiah, but Jeremiah knew God's word was true.

The people put him in a dark pit. Jeremiah cried to God for help.

The people lifted him out of the pit and locked him in jail instead.

But Jeremiah didn't stop warning the people.
  How he wished they would read God's word!
  How he wished they would believe God!
  How he wished they would be kind!
  But the people would not obey God.
  An evil nation did come and fight against them. They captured the people and led them away in chains.
  Jeremiah cried and cried. He was sad because the people would not listen to God.
  He was sad because they would not obey God.
  Many years later the people told God they were sorry. They believed God's truth and returned to their land.

God asked Jeremiah to warn the people of the danger that was coming if they kept on disobeying God. Jeremiah did this for his whole life. But he was sad because the people would not listen and were unkind to him. Still Jeremiah didn't stop.

Who reminds you to obey God and pray to him every day? Your parents? Grandparents? The pastor of your church? Don't be like the people who wouldn't listen to God or to Jeremiah. Always be happy to learn more about God! Always try to please God!

"My lord the king, these men have acted wickedly in all they have done to Jeremiah the prophet. They have thrown him into a cistern, where he will starve to death when there is no longer any bread in the city."

Jeremiah 38:9

WONDER BOOKS
Lessons to learn from 12 Bible characters

God's Love

Self-giving

Prayer Overcomes Fear

Praising God

Prayer Obtains Wisdom

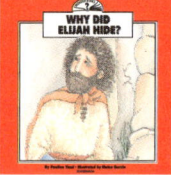

Listening to God

Trust

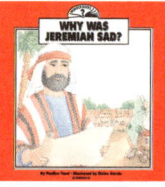

Perseverance

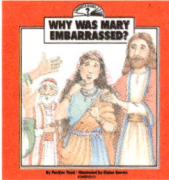

Loving Obedience

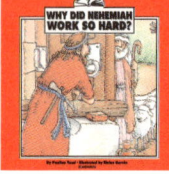

Persistence

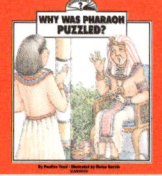

Asking Advice

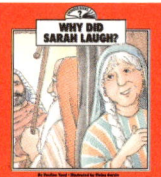

Trusting God's plan